My Thought Stock

Prerna Tiku

BookLeaf Publishing

India | USA | UK

Presentation by *BookLeaf Publishing*

Web: www.bookleafpub.com

E-mail: info@bookleafpub.com

ISBN: 9789360949518

First edition 2024

DEDICATION

To my mother, who is relentlessly loving and unassumingly brave and my daughter, who is refreshingly curious and unbelievably kind.

ACKNOWLEDGEMENT

I want to give a shout-out to all the people, places, musicians and artists who've triggered me to hop on this poetic ride every now and then. To my family for always having my back, to my friends and colleagues for giving me a second home as I step out everyday. I have to especially acknowledge my daughter for helping me re-discover the world all over again. Her questions and curiosity help me see things differently. And to you, dear reader, for choosing to read this theme-less collection of thoughts when you could be scrolling through reels or flipping channels.

PREFACE

Somewhere in the quiet between life and death, where you find yourself on a noisy crossroad of reality and imagination, poetry emerges as a mirror reflecting the complexities of existence. In this collection, you will find pit-stops of a journey, as I watch the world go by from my little window. The inaudible screams of reality and the echoing whispers of dreams that lead up to the synchronized harmony between light and shadow.

Well, poetry is limitless. Every poem that has ever talked to you may have whispered something very different in someone else's ears. I hope these simple words, entangled in somewhat complex thoughts spill everywhere and make a hot mess because only when you sit through this mess, live through the hopes and frustrations of thoughts, will you feel the words and that's all that I wish for.

Sunday

On a warm Sunday morning I laid down on the
grass
Free from all the weight and disease.
Beginning to feel alive, feeling the blades of
grass tickle my wrist.
Closed eyes, my mind took a break from
wandering
But the trapped dreams started to nudge;
Endangered dreams that were starting to feel
breathless.
So I opened one eye and squinted to look up at
the Sun
And she smiled, coz well she made my face look
funny, red cheeks and squinted eyes.
Go back to the world, she said, that is where you
belong,
There are fires to douse and plants to water.

You were born to live, it doesn't matter what
path you choose
Because every path has potholes to fill and
bumps to dodge
So just go find your dream, whisper gently to
your soul and find the smiles,
There are plenty, if you know where to look
So I opened my eyes and set my dreams free
And now they fly around me, close but not
trapped.
Reminding me to live a little better and smile a
little wider, when I can.

Truth

There is no day too long
No storm too strong
No rain too harsh
No sun too sharp
To keep the world from going 'round
We know that isn't true
But we know, we're here
Livin our truth
Fallin on our faces
Recovering and walking again
So just stay...
Stay and feel what I am feeling
Stay and see what I am seeing
Stay and witness the world's imperfections

And smile with me as we see our own
Because life as we know it
Is here, in this very moment
Where you and I exist
Breathing and smiling, sometimes crying
Crying though is a lot like smiling
Just like living is a lot like dying
So let's just be, you and me
Let's stay in this place called here
And watch the world go 'round

Trees and Leaves

Love and hate are the same
never liberated, never controlled.

Prayers and complaints are the same
never selfless, never astute.

Happiness and despair are the same
never sustained, never effervescent.

Madness and sanity are the same
never explained, never understood.

Journey and destination are the same
Never collective, never alone.

Trees and leaves are the same
Never separated, never attached.

Her colourful life (An ode to Emily Dickinson)

She lived her life in dreams
Often rejecting the premise of reality
For her mind wandered places
Forbidden, absurd and confusing.

She lived her life in beliefs
Often believing nothing but her own heart
For her heart thrived on connections
Broken, complex and real.

She lived her life in pain
Often disrupted by strokes of pleasure
For her pain, she treasured dearly
Deep, blinding and colourful.

Life and Death

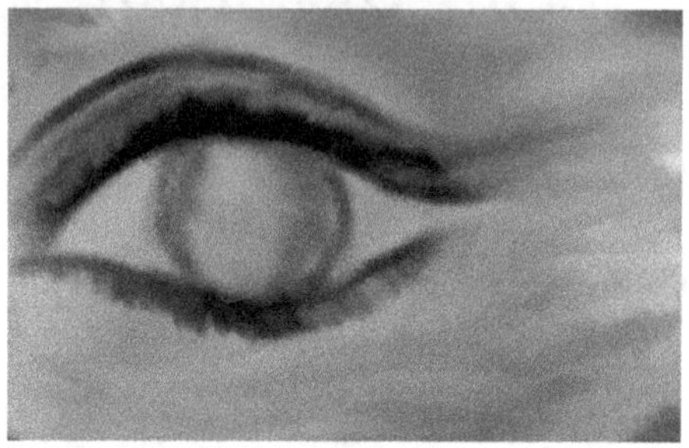

Truncated words, faded feelings,
Shimmering doubt, decomposed healing
Someone said death is the only truth
Don't think they know what's living
Coz one look at life and you know,
No one died by not breathing.

Strangers

Her eyes found his, while he was searching
Strangers sharing a slice of the night
He walked in and she waltzed through
Opening shut doors, just like that!

Her detached glare and her gentle touch
Took him by surprise
His hungry heart and his restless soul
piercing through the empty night

He said, "You can't find me, I am lost"
She shrugged, "I wasn't even looking!"
And yet the dark room was lit
With the afterglow of their seeking

They rested, and fearlessly shared
Their deepest, darkest thoughts without a word!
Healed by the night as the sun rose
Finding something they had never searched!

The morning sun was sharp and strong
As if the night never came
They went their way, never looking back
Remembering the night like a song.

Firewall

Invisible, strong, it stands still
A virtual wall that is built to hunt and kill.
Scans everything wild that tries to enter or leave,
Only allows safe decisions to pass through the
conforming sieve.

Then why, I wonder do my dreams run free?
Pick up every thought and reject every spiel
Question reality and dare to explore
Swim far far away from safe and clean shores.

Dear firewall you're here and that's nice
But I know I will break through and pay the
price
Because no matter how you try to stop or protect
My mind is bonkers and it has its own take.

So go on and save some other treasure
My thoughts are wild, without any measure
You'll be lost and I wouldn't want that
Because you'll need a firewall and that'll be sad.

Your Story

It's crazy, absolutely insane
Twist of fate, and your life was never the same
All that you had in your hand
Just slipped away like loose sand.

People came and people left
What remained is a thought of a song,
the one that you thought you knew too well
But when the words came, you knew you were
wrong

You played the tune over and over again
You sailed through the rain and through the
storm.
Well yes you were always known to be a leader
But did you ever learn to walk alone?

So you just kept going farther and farther away
Searching for the destination and the way
Were you confused, but you said you had it all
figured out
Was there a disconnect between what existed
and what you thought?

It was like uncalled for deja vu
What you needed was selective amnesia
Just to forget to remember the pain
Or relive fond memories again.

Lust for Power

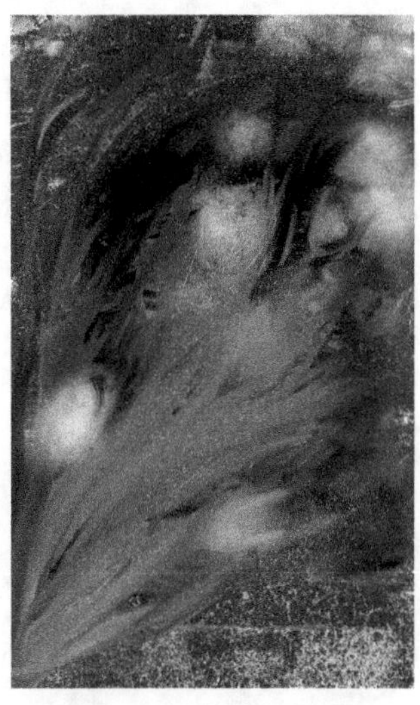

Grabbed the force and held it tight
Holding the crystal of wrong and right
Entangled in the tentacles of power, I hide
Every one sees me but only I, my own guise.

I feel pretty, well-fed on a staple of highs
Crushing all that doesn't fit under my sky
The rush of power play and all that joy
Puppet strings are now my favourite toy.

Don't try digging through my conscience
box of emptiness is all you'll find

I often top it up with charity
And pretend to feel happy inside.

Sometimes at night I hear the quiet screams
My soul in tatters is crying for help
Everything around is make believe
So I ignore and revel in the tragic relief of lies.

Me, you seek! (Music)

Answer when you don't know the question
A maze of thoughts and reflection
Words, that need no language
Sounds that both capture and liberate!

"Eat all you can" buffet for the soul,
Secrets that you only heard but never told
That missing beat of your own heart,
Flashlight when it's pitch dark

Magical mirror mounted on the wall
You look into it and see it all
Memories of childhood, stories that never fade
Journey of life, friends you made

A one-way ticket to the world of dreams
Hidden from the madness, only you can see it.
Music is a religion and that's not all
Will pick you up from the ashes after your
greatest fall.

In Between

A heartbeat takes my breath away
Deep like the belly of the ocean
Wilder than the wind that messes my hair
Just a blink away, waving and calling

We have been here before
Melted and reborn in different shapes and forms
Sleepwalking through unwinding loops of reality
And waking up to dreams in different hues

What makes the rested mind wander?
What brings it peace also triggers its anger

A fractal of imagination that shines
In a bubble bath of stories free yet confined

The poor fragile mind swirls in a flurry
Guilty of joy, pure and pristine
Suspended no more. No anchor, no oars
Weightless and free falling from above

Eventually it will rest in an embrace so warm
Just like the breath it holds within
Finally at peace, finally complete
Never to be lost or found again

Love and Loss

Kissing in the car, watching planes take off
Sleep deprived, young love never stopped
Tug of war between chemistry and ambition
Lost to the life choices, coiled and well strung

Stories, fantasies and dreams on drones
Nameless faces painted on stones
A moderate thunder, few strikes of lightning
Lost to downpour that washed away the tones

Obvious connection, choices in place
Building castles, while running the race
Creating life, finding pieces one by one
Lost to the missing piece, stored by none

Effortless, unfiltered soft rays from the Sun
Honesty, warmth, love, all of it in one
Stuck in boxes, no place for even sound
Lost to the world, left in the box of lost and
found.

Don't Fear the End

Sometimes perfectly packed plans, fail
Your safe was really risk under a veil.

Sometimes to deal with the storm, you've got to
ride the tide
And discover new paths that you never tried

So start again, quit making amends
Every beginning begins, when something ends!

Savitri

Donning the stale garb of happiness
Her tattered restless soul wandered
Stifled by the smell of reality
Comfortable at last in the trenches of the street.

No one listened but everyone heard
Her clap, her bangles but not those silent
screams
Everyone looked but no one saw
The darkness covered by that bright red lipstick.

Faces turned in disgust and anger
Almost ashamed of her very existence
Her fading voice amidst honking cars
Never helpless, always proud!

She walked with grace I had never seen
Blessing generously every hand that stretched
Even though all she asked for
Was some change and respect.

"What's your story Savitri", I wondered
As she told me her name.
She used words I couldn't understand
And yet we spoke everyday.

30 seconds of smiles and acknowledgement
And then we would go our way
And then one day, I stopped as usual
But she wasn't there...

I wonder as I drive away everyday,
"What's your story Savitri" I hope you're safe.

She

Her children, they go to school
She feels proud as they walk out with their
school bags
She feels proud of her resolve too!

She ties her well-oiled hair into a bun
Covers her hardened heels with slippers
Covers her disappointment too!

She steps out of her humble truth
Everyday, into the world of wide skies and long
roads
Everyday she cleans houses too!

She rings the doorbell a few times
Waits till it is answered
Waits for her prayers to be answered too!

She returns home every night
Tired and hungry
Tired of her struggles too!

What is her fault she wonders
As she finds her savings box on the floor
As she finds her drunk husband on the floor too

She feeds her young children
Puts them to bed, humming a tune
Puts her dreams to bed too

You're not Welcome

This is not an answer, but it's not even a
question.
Some unexpected turns, make you question your
action.

Tickled by life itself and its sneaky little ways
You try to control everything and all its charades

Sometimes you know that you can't really
control
And yet you keep fighting and ignore that tiny
hole

The one that built slowly inside on a dose of
self-doubt
Grew with negativity building a hard clout

Control, now that's a tricky word isn't it?
It's not everyday that you feel like you fit

Wait, isn't it your life though?
Shouldn't you make the rules and others stand in
tow?
There, did I just mess up your head a bit more?
Don't hesitate to access your own choice, to shut
that door....

...on every negative thought, every degenerative
comment.
What pierced through doesn't have the power to
leave a dent.

Unless you open that door and invite it in
But remember leaving un-invited guests out was
never a sin!

Dream Dead Gorgeous

Blanket of grey with flashes of light
Right through the glass, you see the blue sky
Just footsteps away, the blinding blur makes its
way
The whiff of air that almost takes your breath
away.

Through half-open blinds, sparkle the lonely
tears
What the heart wants is what the mind fears
Dreams, they swim tirelessly back to the shore
They are safe you know, tucked in that secret
store!

Oh the brilliance of the fire is striking
You look closer something dear is burning
The store is on fire, with darkness wrapped all
around
The silence is deafening but don't hear a sound.

And then the darkness fades into the day
Ruins of dreams mingled with the ashes stay
Crashing into the walls of the fragile soul
Mocking at moments, laughing like a droll.

That filled up urn of ashes and dreams you just
sold...
What did you get when you sold your soul?

Cupcakes and Strangers

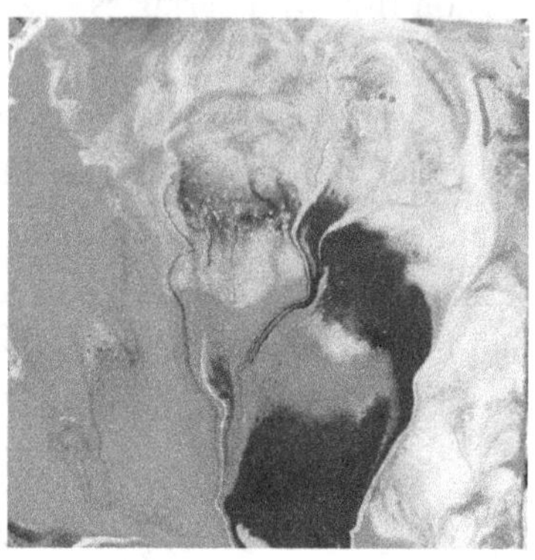

Batter full of awesomeness, it stares
Waiting for you, for no one else is here
The answer is simple, but can you really see
You struggle to hold the whisk and beat
What stops you from taking the plunge, to care

Is it your fears that ask you to steer clear?
You thought risk is in getting it all wrong
Even though it's as easy as humming a song.
So you see someone out there picked it up
Whisked it well and filled their cup

They were afraid but they were aware
They failed but they didn't really care
"A thing of beauty is a joy forever"
Maybe you're a fool and they are clever?

You always took the tough way out
Hardships made you happy and so proud
Remember, life only gives a few cupcakes
And there is always a stranger who knows how
to bake!

Contradictions

Walk, for nowhere is where you need to go
Talk, for no one who's around will ever know
Dance, for there's no music you hear till very far
Show, for everything you conceal will make you
a star!

Feeding the Ego

Shimmer of the past and blur of the future
Relentlessly trying and fanatically brutal
Striving for a vision but blinded by the glow
Marching right ahead but dreading the blow

All about winning, game of tic-tac-toe
Staging every moment, never hearing 'no'
Engineering a new reality of only rights
Hounded by the wrongs on cold and lonely
nights

The goal that drove me is now just a petty dot
I love what I am, what I think and what I want

Today is not that Day

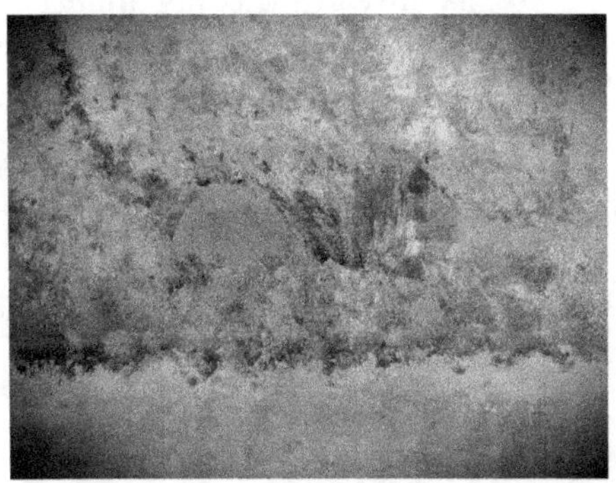

There are days my resolve is strong
My smile is wide
And my voice is clear
There are days I make sense
But today is not that day.

There are days I see glass half full
My mind unwinds slow
My hands bring out beauty
I see the world and its glow
But today is not that day.

There are days I can hear your voice
I can see your story
Music too finds its way
And thoughts always connect
But today is not that day.

There are days I accept my flaws
My voids and my cracks
My inability to speak my mind
And impulse to say things I don't mean
But today is not that day

There are days I feel like I have changed
Become practical and plain
Not entangled in ropes of thoughts
Free from retrospection and pain
But today... is not that day.

Doorway

No matter how much water goes through the
spring
Don't be afraid, let the darkness in

Underwater, through the tunnel of pain,
Find the doorway that remains.

Never before and never again,
Will your heart talk to your brain

So grab that moment and jump ahead
The wide-eyed you has far been dead!

Only Fools

My steps follow the sound that I struggle to
ignore.
It's not a voice, it's not a face, it's a feeling.
That's building in the deep of my heart
I know shadows of the past can appear anytime!
And the darkness could swallow me whole.
And yet...
And yet my hand reaches out to find
the answers my heart demands to have!

For centuries, generations have known...
Only to wake up to a tomorrow that's planned
for them.
A tomorrow that's just like today and a today
that was planned yesterday.

And maybe you can live like that everyday for
the rest of your life.
But can you ignore the sound that travels
through you when you care to listen?
Maybe it's wise to do that and foolish to disturb
the balance.

But fools, my sweet, are not afraid to be foolish.
They know the world has vested interest in
perceived balance of offered choices.
Because creativity really doesn't worry about
rules that control our lives.
Losing control is probably the scariest thing for
anyone!
But really ask yourself this, are you in control or
being controlled?

Woman

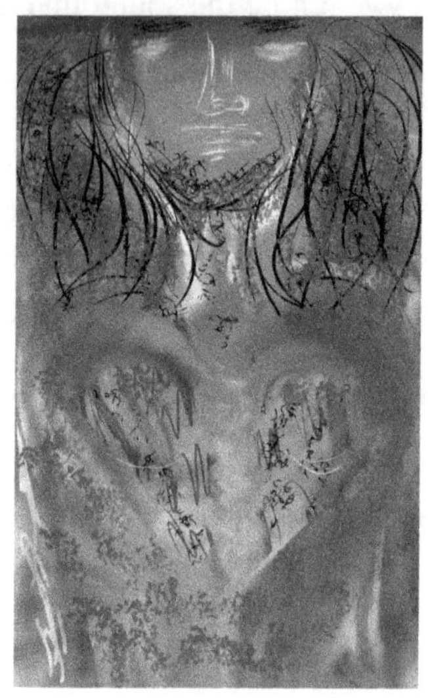

She smiles, she cries
She celebrates, she hurts
She walks, she falls
She burps, she farts
She's not special
She needn't be celebrated
Let her be human
So don't remind her of her gender
Remind her of her strength
Don't tell her she's a superwoman
Just tell her she's not alone
Don't ask her to smile for you

Ask her to speak for herself
Don't tell her she's perfect
Tell her that she's safe
Don't celebrate a day for her
Celebrate life!

Crash Land

In my bottomless bowl of imagination,
I collected the strangeness of my mind

Taking a dip in that chilling pool,
A journey is what I find!

In an unexpected piece of peace,
A blinding light appeared
Relax! the dream wasn't over yet
But reality got pretty fierce

I stood still, as my choices began to speak
One said "yay!" while the other one just freaked!

Out of control, the wind was running wild
I held my choices tightly like a small child

Regret pulled me back, claiming to be my friend
Saying there was still time, if I could just stretch
out my hand...

It could keep me safe even though I may never
really stand
But I chose to fly even if I had to Crash Land!

I woke up with a jolt, in a misty haze.
Was it just a dream that I was trying to chase?

It was dark but something inside me just lit up
I had to get up, I had to sit up

If this was reality why did the dream feel so real
I couldn't contain anymore, I couldn't conceal

So I got up, stretched and started to walk
I didn't care what people would say or talk

Coz building a dream was a choice, not a
mystery
So I walked ahead and didn't get stuck in history.

Pinned down!

Sometimes the only person you fight is yourself.
This way or that, it's you who bites the dust!
No strategies, no clever tricks, no one-ups.
You know yourself so it's hard to pretend.
And yet you do!
You lie to yourself, you cheat, you try to fool but
eventually...
Who can hide from their own shadow?

Even if you do your best to keep the room dark.
The thing about turning your back on light is
that the shadow is the largest
when the light is behind you.
Your demons amplify, as if to swallow your
whole self!

And then the pins of regret appear.
Tiny, like ants, seemingly insignificant
You think, they are just pins what can they do?
But every tip pierces through
Puncturing the bubble you built.
You can't find a safe corner even if you try.
Because those tiny holes, millions of them are
everywhere!
So drenched, you ask yourself
"Who am I and how did I get here?"

Unspoken

Oh stray thoughts, you are innocent
Stopping by when I am sleeping, to check on me
They blame you for my sleepless nights
But you make me dream, what do they know?
Oh stray thoughts, you are harmless
Smiling as I long for a warm touch on cold
nights
They blame you for my loneliness
But you keep me company, what do they know?
Oh stray thoughts, you are my friend
Dancing with me, wild and crazy
They blame you for my madness,
But you keep me sane, what do they know?

And oh stray thoughts, finally at peace
In the quiet of nothingness, enveloped in grief
No one can blame you, when they don't see me.
So oh stray thoughts finally, it's just you and me!

Waking Life

Surrounded by the sound of silence
I lay in my bed
My restless emotions go backpacking through
my soul and say
"Keep walking for no one shares your journey"
"Keep walking, you're not alone there have been
many"
So I reach out for the door and look for a sign
Is it a "push" or a "pull" I wonder, standing in
time!
I hesitate but something draws me closer

I take a step towards the voice that calls me
over!

It says, "There is someone who knows you
inside out
You haven't met her but you already like her a
lot.
It is a tiny piece of your own soul
and that piece makes her soul whole!
So discover that piece, don't let it go
Write a story, no matter where you go".
Empty handed I finally take the first step...
No plan, no design and just nothing to fret!

Cut the cliché

Sunk in her book, she couldn't care less
He walked past her but knew not to mess
She opened the door and there he was
He smiled at her but she didn't pause
A broken heart she was trying to mend
She was not looking for a lover but only a
friend.

Poems or Lovers

String of words sometimes comes alive
Like long lost lovers destined to meet
Stretched breaths of imagination appear
Wrapped in a strange kind of joy
Like two intertwined inseparable souls
that were waiting for stars to align,
Words and thoughts come together
Swimming through the conduit of spilled tears
And then the inevitable happens
The joy explodes, breaking into a million stars
Finding its way to the deepest and darkest parts
Till everything is lit and everything is revealed

Why

Why must I say when I can write
Why must I hurt when I can fight
Why must I talk when I can sing
Why must I fear when I can think
Why must I run when I can fly
Why must I give up when I can try
Why must I endure when I can scream
Why must I dread when I can dream

www.ingramcontent.com/pod-product-compliance
Lightning Source LLC
La Vergne TN
LVHW050933200726
843508LV00011B/2338